Dedications

as a young child

I knew in one sudden moment

my destiny-

to share my stories

in any way I could and

through any opportunity,

not due to egotistical vanity

but because of my experiences' variety

and their Affinity

with Humanity

for my daughter, family, dear friends and all fellow empaths- especially ones attempting to break free of either societal chains and categorizations, or narcissistic abuse of one kind or another.

-Sel[1]

---

[1] Means *"your flood"* in Turkish. Author's nickname.

Dear beloved reader:

Yes, *you*. If this collection has found its way to you, then I believe you to be an empathetic soul with many drops to pour into the globally-connective oceans as the collective human race.

This, dear reader, makes you beloved- and more valuable than you know.

I had written many of these poems before the onset of the tragic pandemic. In retrospect, I find that some of them about the new year and nature have eerily been foreboding. I sincerely hope these words find you and your loved ones in good health, and my heartfelt condolences to those of you whose loved ones were more negatively impacted.

The verses on these pages range from the very personal to the very objective, and as an observer of abstract art like in 'The Ballerina's Catalysis' and 'Tropical Loss'.

My own name, Selin, translates to "your flood" in Turkish. As a believer in the universe somehow symbolically always trying to tell us something, I hope you can smile along with me in my love of play-on-words throughout the pages.

May your flood of teardrops, sweat drops, melodic art and the blood flowing through your veins all unite and rain onto the connecting oceans as your fluid imprints. I encourage you to express your own universal vision, and bleed out your art and stories.

Write out your drops. Write out your world.

xOxO

SSA

Drops of Precipitation............7

Drops of Tears............28

Drops of Perspiration............65

Drops of Music............94

Drops of Blood............127

the dandelion

the winds of change
have begun to blow
even mightier than the unusual
rainy summer winds
of this already most unusual, viral year

the winds of change have shattered any
proximity in clinging to routines
and familiar daily visions and habits

they have caused an additional conundrum
at a time when long-hauled weights
had been begging to be finally released
from aching shoulders

it is said we take ourselves wherever we go
country to city, city to country
alone to partnered, partnered to alone
burdened to relieved, relieved to burdened

the cycle never truly ceases
as long as we're alive
the change itself may indeed be
the only fuel needed
to carry and drive on by

fate only exists to a certain point
after which you must decide
your own form of high

are you rooted to grow your flowers,
risking rotting?
or
a dandelion
enjoying being blown along with the wind?

the value of the flower

valuable

never realized
what has truly been
invaluable
until the virus made all of us
vulnerable

a glance from a mask
a touch on the hand
a question you're able to ask
over only forced broadband

hoping someday to understand
the purpose of it all

the suffering you suppress
you progress, then regress

praying for some salvation
before the last curtain call
before we take that big fall

all the world's a stage
had said the theatrical sage

on these emptier streets
full now of discarded gloves and masks
whether or not tomorrows
can still be promised
the blooming flower never asks

penitent souls

the ways of the past
could not possibly last
we knew the inevitable truths
we still ignored
thinking this generation
would be exempt from
the globe's defiant blast

Mother Nature was always
the force to be reckoned with
even more powerful than love
in regards to both beauty and pain
she coughed a contagious poison
global warming and our sins weren't myth

we try now to repent
living more simply and whole
holding down our families & forts
when we cannot even hold or shake
the hands of outsiders
lest we risk losing it all

let's apologize to nature encompassing the
trees and sky we see
as well as to the Being and Creator
that we don't

let's apologize also to our spirit
for seeking temporary outside validation
when we knew all along our duties
to maintain its purity

bodies may die
but souls won't

pessimistic optimism

seasons come and go
the phrase has become
as cliché
as a winter with snow

this city that
doesn't sleep
hasn't seasonably witnessed
much of it lately though

the new year
has indeed commenced
after everyone clinked
their glasses
and danced for hope
with a January
catalyzing global trauma
instead

we've still got much to concern
ourselves with
I'm afraid
up ahead

resilience

surveying the damage
after Isaias
the weather eerily wet and warm
catalyzed her to survey the damage
of the past year as well:
trying to salvage any good she can
from the remnants of the storm

teardrops, year after year
increasingly cease
from free-falling
and rather lump up in the throat
after betrayal and strife
with hidden shameful mourning

they call it experience and maturity
she hides that it's necessary adaptability

majestic trees
now merely unrooted debris
lie sideways as a neighbor takes a selfie

she, too, is at times defeated
by Mother Nature
yet resilience
is also *her* best feature

daisies

Winter can take you
by surprise
with a sudden and inconvenient
slap of frost
when you'd been expecting a longer Fall
with lingering moments of warmth
still not lost
allow Summer to reign
inside your heart
disregarding the cold pain of memories
Spring will surely return once again
blossoming hopes
alongside the daisies

esteem

it's a mother's nature
to care for and nurture
until fatigue sets in
and patience runs thin
in which case we turn into
a most angry creature

Mother Nature gave us bliss
the loveliest scents and sights
but we did not value its glory
so, it released its viral fury
now what we can no longer do
we miss

so, please, tell me this:
when can we ask for forgiveness?
when can we again have her mercy?
before all mothers
let us show courtesy

one-sided

with the sun comes expectations
warmth for our skin
healing from within
our heart beats faster with palpitations
hormones kick in
let the summer begin
no one considers the sun's sensations
or the one-sided duty it's performing
aiding you with warmth
no matter who you've been

redeem

why is it
that the beautiful sun
peeks out
from the clouds
just as the day is ending?

why is it
that the hurtful lover
with the shout
only succumbs
to softness
just as the relationship
is past mending?

why is this
human nature?
can we redeem ourselves
to enjoy what we can
while we are able?

let's ponder
and enjoy the sun
not thunder

lunar

it's not that the moon
doesn't hurt or care
but she knows how to share
the message that to truly shine
it must also persevere through
solo moments of despair

the moon exists in the day yet
doesn't shine as brightly
as it does nightly
just remains rather gray
and instead
allowing the way
for the sun to keep the cold away

the tree and the forest

to be like a tree
rooted deep
yet swaying from time to time
without falling over

surrounded by beings to whom you can relate
and trust
in order to coexist with you
without needing to glance
over your weary shoulder

unlike us
trees can trust
no worries of rust

reawakening

when a flower is stomped on
it tilts
its will crushed
it wilts
with every disappointing, darkened shade
the once-beating Red
goes through a fade

the flowers decorate the yard
as the thoughts of you surround
my daily ponderings
I contemplate what you're doing right then
at a particular moment

just as I wonder
when exactly did the petals
on that blush-pink peony fall off?
when did our occasionally-watered rose wither?

how did those other roses,
in that other corner
unexpectedly bloom?
I'd lost all hopes on those white ones

yet there they are: fluffily adorned in spring
no- I decide
I shan't yet let go hope of what our own
reawakening
may bring

shade

clouds are underrated
without them
the sky is an infinite yet eerie shade of *blue*
reaching the vast unknown cosmos

yet clouds exist only to hydrate our lives
on the proud, *green* and *brown* earth
we are special to the clouds
a fact overlooked by most

but which shade art thou?
are you a *red*, instead?

closer to *orange*- like a scorching flame?
in proximity to light *pink*- of sweetheart fame?
a darker fuchsia, befitting a classy dame?
or, are you more Cardinal
like the Sin

do you too err in judgement
after which nothing
can remain the same?

with each sunset, our cheeks blush
a different shade of rose
whether innocently or of shame

the clouds, however, never falter
hydration and shade- their only game

floral grace

petals, too, can fall from grace
tossed over a bride after the ceremony
settling on the concrete ground
after brushing her made-up face
having once been rooted to a stem
which in turn clung proudly for life
deep inside the charcoal earth

they stood dainty yet strong under the sun
to think, they could now be hurled like trash
a prism of splendid hues
lustrous still despite being used
a confetti of true allure
cannot be handled by everyone

the rain's joy

with the rain
comes expectations
of cozy sweaters tickling the skin
and other such sensations

not too hot, not too cold
catalyst October
is rather quite bold

after old leaves have been shed
new opportunities can be bred
unlike us, the joy from traversing crunchy leaves
never grows old

with each chilly breeze
you get weak in the knees
like a warm cardigan
or a wondrous kiss
Autumn holds bliss

pumpkin spice & everything nice
with routines and habits
there's no need to think twice

living ordinarily but standing out
through true happiness
grandiosity can feel amiss
simple joys sometimes just have to suffice

Drops of Tears

the offspring

what happens to love
when the relationship that formed it
is in turmoil?

does it weep, too, along with the lover
like a helpless child
or burn like petrol oil?

can it be transmitted to the next lover
like a stepchild, pet, or plant
despite missing its original soil?

perhaps that love will always live on
in infinity and beyond
in memory- a baby you can never spoil

the gazelle

what good is it
being the pursuit
when all it leaves you with
is less spirit than before
life had already taken a toll on her heart
before the hunter aimed the arrow
straight to the core
by the fragile bone marrow
exuding control
she held on to her art
while distracted
by persuasive suggestions
to let go of it all

after its energy has been stolen
or compromised:
does the bear- left without life
feel flattered
that it has been the Hunter's prize?

she was convinced
to lower her shield for social gain
ultimately the thrills, though
were never worth the pain

she should have seen
through the front
from the always
dubious start

the trophy
was both the game and the prize
and once obtained
it'd be placed
high on a shelf
collecting dust
never cared for
from then on
merely smiled upon
as a memory
though it'd long been left
to rust

the shield breaker

when he coyly smiled at her
a few seconds longer than the rest
her willpower to combat forbidden love
had at once been put to the test

when he boyishly wrote to her
a few verses more personal than others
her brain sensed a rush, and thought
this love frees, more than it smothers

when he nervously held her hand
with a few extra kisses, like a princess
her soul could never predict
that soon all would become a mess

when he purposely halted his chase
cursing their speculated fate
her tears transformed from drops
into a sea of enamored hate

lay versus lie

lay all your cards on the table
you've been too good at
bluffing
too good at Poker

taking off your proud mask
shouldn't be such a difficult task
be my Batman
don't be Joker

let's lie down, watch the stars
don't think about taking it there for once
let's ponder something
that can become an inside joke instead
like, 'what if we were living on Mars?'

I too desire the kisses on fire
and that firm grip, oh my
but this time lay your heart on the line
and promise
not to lie

shout

why look above
for affirming signs
of what you already know from inside out?

why deny a love
which you can
but do not want to live without?

why distance an embrace
when it leaves a smile on your face?

do you hide from the soul's request
and risk a permanent pout?
or mount yourself on a proverbial
mountaintop or rooftop
and simply let it out?

shout

diamond in the rough

to feel the sting of sin
upon our moral scale of the self
like unread yet most attractive, clean books
full of colors and verses
of the most-descriptive hooks
grabbed and devoured
abruptly from the shelf

a demure sense of emotion
set off-balance by a desire set in motion
a pure sense of duty
set ablaze with heat sparked in the body

what good is love
if left to rot inside?
what good is a diamond
if it must always hide?

the unloving flatterer

what good does
constant flattery
inflict
when you see the roving eye
more than you care to admit
in order to avoid
conflict?

when the lover
simply loves beauty
it isn't the true you
they forever seek
but rather continuously
chasing images
in which to find
their *perfect*

when you're made to feel
truly special
for all that you are
within and throughout
that is the one your soul
won't question
and give its all for

if it's you
they don't want to live without
your heart to them
will remain
devout

love on a diet

it starts off as grand as the universe
an explosion of fire in the heart
and stars in the eyes
tender sweetness spilling from the lips

it then loses weight
like flowers drinking water
less and less frequently
bulging love handles gradually withering away
revealing thinner hips

love of passion finally remains
a skeleton of what once was
sometimes glorious like an ancient mummy
still holding onto some of its old teeth and hair
other times- completely rotted and bare
unaware
of the stare
from the soul that had once also been there

upon the discovery of a hole
love drips and dips

the bee vs. the fly

the humble yet exquisite flower
can never deny its nectar
which despite their large amounts of fear
pulls those verbose-when-enamored near

tell me, oh amorous being in the sky
are you ultimately a pesky little fly
just interested in a temporary feed or high?

or a bee- buzzing royally nearby
with intent to receive benefit
but give it as well?
don't lie

dependence

patterns
are good to knit
patterns
are good to raise a kid
routines mean expecting
habits are humbling
when the world outside
is thundering
settling is
soothing &
trusting

until it's not

until patterns abuse
until habits misuse
patterns can be hard
to break
but some must be broken
before they break
your self-respect
and boundary rules
be your own officer
and dignity defender
your own muse

illicit

you and the lover
are on the same boat
don't forget

remember the law of karma
before you take an action
you'll eventually regret

your feisty eyes
burn the soul of the other
a blooming surprise
of emotions flood the ether

catch them as they fall
without a promise of safety
a dangerous love affair
isn't worth it at all

for even the strongest of flames
get put off by the winds of time
and tides of change
when future possibilities
are small

escape

after a certain point
you've learned
upon countless experience miles
you've earned

that being smart is different from
acting smart
a dubious, tell-tale start
disguised as art
kind words for convenient gain
don't equate to having a heart

that forgiveness and appreciation
aren't always reciprocated
sometimes you're stuck doing
what you once swore you hated

that imploring eyes
can best disguise
a wolf in sheep's clothing
full of narcissistic lies

no one is perfect
and neither are you
yet if you've done all you could
what's done was at least true

flying in chains

though contemplation takes hold
on a daily basis
as the hours pass on by
there are some things
I still cannot fathom

people get hurled and chastised
unappreciated when you've actually got 'em

and the blood in our veins
said to be thicker than water
can pump more painfully
when expectations are forced
rather than whatever comes naturally

another birthday has arrived
with much still lost
despite several gains

momentous occasions
to distract from the unpleasantly- packaged gift
of recognizing the cold truth of our chains

the exception

the sun has set
its view is surely gone
and we cannot get it back
though we are still lucky
and must consider ourselves so
for we've caught it
and we still see the traces
of purple tinges in the sky
as two French boys on bikes
speed on by
and we'll always have its trace
in memories
never underestimating, though
that we've actually caught it
as well
the *it* many search for
the sunset by the lake
swinging with your hand in mine
glances intertwined
perfection

the ballerina's catalysis

she rushes backstage after her abrupt exit
bursting into the tears long held back
there they are, she spots them
on her changing-room counter
his final bouquet, she presumes
congratulations, the note indeed begins
yours always in heart, with immense pride, it stops

she chuckles with disgust
it appears the note too has an unexpected start
and a short end

the image of his chiseled face in the audience
will not leave her mind
his stare- intense and green
as the leaves in the vase
his firm hands- his left one in particular
had been holding on to the small of her back
just last week as they'd been strolling
amongst giggles in the park

it was now being covered by her right hand
the sparkling on her right finger visible
and blinding from the front row
so the woman had received the present
she'd been waiting for after all
though not his heart

or perhaps she had received that as well
and it was only this ballerina who had been fooled

no longer
actions were the thing
words were futile, she'd forcibly learned
"CRACK!"

braver

after it's over
you lean back on the pillows
and turn your head toward the window
the curtains quiver in the soft wind
in waves as the pleasures in my body
had just been

after it's over
you no longer light your cigarette
you quit with my help
though I could not quit you

clichés were never your thing either
never a candlelit dinner getaway
or flowers for a lady in May

after it's over
you lose yourself in your soulless
skin-driven life
without any intention of making
or keeping a wife
swearing you never want to be
like the father you'd never known
yet didn't he too cause many
immeasurable strife?

after it's over
you're stuck in your darkness still
swearing that it causes you glee
this quality of being forever
unattached and free

after it's over
my wounds have still yet to close
but the one who loves wholeheartedly
is the real winner through and through

I'm braver than you

four seasons of a beautiful betrayal

in that moment
when the first dawn rays hit
my humble room
I often reflect back on our days
of viscous Summer together
to appease my gloom

Spring in New York is the loveliest in the world
it is said
surpassed only by the allure of its Fall

I loved you
despite all of your seasons and intricate flaws
with your harsh brutal Winter
of sharp icicles on my back and all

tropical loss

the tropics with my beloved
I shall never forget
though to this day, I must admit
I live on with some regret

I wore my linen dress, long and flowing
as free as a canary in the wind
my hair had been pulled up high
on the top of my head
to avoid that sweat to the skin

let's reproduce right here on this island
he'd said, ever the romantic
we've got all the time in the world
I'd responded
don't be so dramatic

the vessel took us that afternoon
to the shimmering coastal shores
we'd signed up on a whim

the sunset took my beloved
away from me
a part of me too drowned there
right along with him

acquiescence

science tells us that heaviness
sets to the ground
while the lightness floats

yet it is your evil
that still haunts me and hovers
around my ceiling the most

how many souls had your charcoal spirit
already trapped?
when upon my heart's wall door
you'd stumbled
and rather so loudly tapped?

must this lingering haunting
be my punishment for believing?
must I awake still with nightmares
despite still tearing up with yearning
for you every other evening?

I shall long for your love no longer
and only desire now to exorcise
your memory's malice and venom

yet if your malevolent spooks leave
without my conciliation
would they not take me too with 'em?

roller coaster

to the one who cried love
who'd seemed at first
to have been sent from above
a savior from the routine
a daily switch to either lift my spirits
or sink them to the pit of my stomach
never anything in between

my reason to start my day
to dress up my hours and face
even when I'd been feeling quite gray

you return now to cry love once more
just as I'd finally boarded another ship
away from your rocky shore

do I board your roller coaster?
self-control
is something I still have yet to master

deny

amorously, eventually
I fall
you deny making me
I react
you deny provoking me
on your Hunter's lies
I choke
you deny overfeeding me
with my last remaining
ounce of sanity and strength
I run away

and deny you

the clown fisherman

the foolish clown
at first impression
follows around the queen missing her crown
breathing life into her silent depression

my savior by fate
she now opines
with surprising admiration

not realizing that the minute it's reeled in some
fishermen can hurl the fish
right back into the ocean

lost ones merely crave the attention
of an undeniably prestigious spirit
craving first for their dark soul to gain recognition
only to later back-off of purity:
with a heart never truly in it

the unfrequented sin

you were a country I hadn't frequented before
I got lost without a map along the rocky shore
you approached wise beyond your years
I'd never seen a face so fierce
until my heartbreak fed your ego more

you're too good for me
was the line that'd reeled me in
made me feel safe along your translucent skin

I envy your thorough preparation, though
you knew the precise point at which to let me go

I just wish I'd known in advance, too, before the sin

a cut of you

cut it out
your humor hurts
and the words linger

cut it off
your long hair
has witnessed much anger

cut it out
your heart's shape
from a paper of color

cut in
any fake conversation you may see
between myself and another

and give me that part of you to keep
I'll swallow it into somewhere deep
your heart will remain in me forever

belittled

with every sunset
her externally inflated expectations of love
disappear too
like the sun's rays
little by little

expectations can only
genuinely
be raised internally

an organic feeling of faith
in a union's future
that either exists
or doesn't really

she shall finally grow up
the age of her spirit
may still be little
but it must not
accept being belittled

the mermaid's selective memory

only the waves of good memories
were allowed to wash over me
the cold truths were kept at bay
waves of bad memories
didn't make it to the shore

but don't forget
I'm a Mermaid
I can swim galore

when you need it again
the most
I will
actively and purposely
not love thee anymore

clueless disgrace

we borrow hearts
and lend our own
like library books
away on temporary loan

we unknowingly rent out
our arms to embrace
only to let go with the homeowner's return
attempting to then save face

whether we're acting in love
something innocent, or taboo
our minds can tell us one thing
while the hearts don't have a clue

the phantom of the library

borrowed hearts, you're unable to own
like library books, away on temporary loan
I'd once written, romantically
they've since been tossed
though once a possibility
to now mourn

my pleas- went to deaf ears
my tears- ignored by blind eyes
without healing the roots to grow
by the flower, you were mesmerized

with each word
I walked on eggshells
my unvalued love became suppressed
along with my inability to speak
as I wept silently, to avoid yells

lasting love between opposites
is a myth
and gold can best be appreciated
only by a goldsmith

and my heart- sinking to the bottom
my jokes- you barely even got 'em
allow me to now sing my goodbye
and borrow from the Phantom

and all the cries I may have shed
for this twisted fate
have now turned cold, and into
tears of hate

proposals

make me an offer
one that can't be refused
for promises have been broken
and good intentions, overused

with opportunities given trampled
enthusiasm has finally dampened

yet I still want to believe
it's the truth you wear on your sleeve

Drops of Perspiration

mata hari

World War Three exists
every season
between my heart, my body
and my sense of reason
I attempt
foolishly
to mediate
yet I can never quite satiate
nor could I ever concentrate
when my tears for all three casualties
fall quite often
when I cannot choose
I am often imprisoned
for
treason

psychology

there's apparently a void in me
I discovered it in therapy
which I fill with anyone and anything
to avoid facing that feeling of 'empty'

yet I'm not a gas tank
must get my alone time back
no toxic cycles repeated
just for a good month or so
for too many times
my heart cracked and sank

maybe Freud said it best
a girl abandoned by her father
can't fully feel whole
in peace may he rest

mental curse

to fall into the abyss
whether by
tripping, jumping, or
being thrown
but still survive
after being magnetically
pulled to the bottom core
into that land unknown

you sling right back up
like a shooting star
in reverse
try to maintain
your positivity
and sanity
through a forced smile
or a verse

many can't truly know
how mental suffering
can be a curse
yet like Disney Princesses
with their own
some curses disguise
blessings
behind the scenes
shown

walking in the urbanite's shoes

city life
isn't always opportunities and lights
this morning on the train
it's disgusting smells, sounds, and sights

the proverbially greener pastures
on the other side
they too rot without daily care
life can bore you
slower than a tortoise at times
only to later shake you to the core
and grab you by the hair

beauty isn't always as happy
and together as it appears
you'll never know when, inside
strife has struck its youth
and has added rapid years

a friendly greeting
becomes a facade
a way to hide
all the kryptonite
of the urbanite

settlements

to be settled
wise elders say
is cozier than excitement

a house that's familiar
a home despite its flaws
an imperfectly familiar companion
a ring that made them yours

children to settle into bed
or a pet you're snuggling
truly are lovelier predicaments
as long as you're not settling

the undeceivable one

the cheater on quizzes
and later on lovers

becomes eventually
a most surprising addition
to the world of mothers

she sinks and rises
before being thrown overboard again
and later hovers

floating above the water
in a realm of limbo
more heated than heavenly
she must not cheat, her child, though
from precious fleeting time with her company

the cheater must remember
a child's memory in retrospect
is one that rarely falters

a mother's humility

the best gifts I've received
were painfully harsh
and brutally cold
life lessons

depression
only comes to visit
from time to time now
she strikes suddenly
not in waves of longer
seasons

the angel of purpose and pure light
shines before my eyes daily
so brightly

if it weren't for her
of golden brown curls
I would be lost
when faced with what evil hurls

a poet's best friend

poetry weaves a web of protection
on the poet's emotions

allows us to feel both universal support
and acceptance of our fluid devotions

come what or who may
the verses will lay
in their realm
for a read or write
awaiting

they can never leave us either
our mutual interdependence quivers
anticipating

innocence lost

blue
I'm blue
a young girl wrote
once upon an adolescent time
feeling stuck on these same old emotions like glue
she'd continued
she did always love to rhyme

I'm a bird trapped in my cage
she'd also written
yearning to break free
like I could, long before
harsh realities in this world began to follow me

her heart was pure, her rage was raw
she'd witnessed things no child
should ever say they saw

how was she to know then
that a child would one day hold her hand
and that child would have a doll named *Blue?*

how was she to know then
that that child's father would indeed
become that caged bird
despite his innocence
and after the great injustice which had occurred?

I know that my wings will mend and I can fly again
she'd begun the last verse
of her high-school-published ballad
though it will never be the same
she concluded
a conclusion which to this day remains valid

for following the storms
her rainbows have indeed appeared
but they can never be luminous
just rather pallid

the poet's fidelity

don't fall in love with a poet
you'll be disappointed before you know it
yes, you'll feel at first
immortal
as a subject in their verses'
portal
but we are more enamored with
love
than a human
beloved

the giver

it is excruciating
to be misunderstood
when understanding
is the goal of your livelihood

different from
culturally-set norms
since childhood
I've stood out alone
some praised this
others never could

I blush- it is not shyness
I've just been raised
with manners and kindness

I love- it is not meekness
I smile when I can make another smile
this is my habit- not weakness

resolutions

can newness
fill in
the deficiencies
left over
from the past?

can novelty
erase away
prior mistakes
so their effects
don't last?

can the New Year
human-invented, not of nature
have the power of healing?

does it really matter
though
when it's all in our
states of mind?
so never stop trying
and living
ignore that we're born
simply for dying

the great forgiver

who determines what we deserve?
destiny?
where is the freedom
to choose?
moral versus immoral reactions to pain?
can we pretend to win, when we lose?

no one can judge
if they have not been in the other's shoes
and faced the exact type
of excruciating loneliness

only when I can't forgive
but judge myself
that's when God has judged as well
though I believe in His eventual
forgiveness

years

15 candles
on her birthday cake
she didn't know the direction
her forced-to-bloom-early life would take

25 was the milestone
they'd said
it didn't have to be your dream job as
long as you'd gotten paid

35 still holds promise
as it reluctantly nears
this time she's more realistic
made wiser through her tears

day-to-day

avoid sustaining
a pout
whenever life throws a curveball
your way

whether apathetic
or devout
holding on to pain
will be your
downfall
however often
you pray

living with
regret
must not be
a safety net

own well-intentioned
choices
respect those
voices
in your head

any day could be the last
brave each sunset

true

tame your ego
not your
hopes
squander expectations
that wound you up in
ropes

style your soul
to your maximum
best
without rehearsals
of
fake verses
to pass someone else's
test

like a fingerprint or snowflake
uniqueness
can sometimes be more
than what they can take

whenever you feel reflective
there's always an alternate perspective
stay true to you- don't be fake

the fewer, the truer
commit to being you
and the true
will commit too

the north star

feast your eyes upon
the loveliest star-subjective
out there on the horizon
never stop to think
whether it'd always shone as bright each and every
previous season

when it's shining, you're smiling
when it's shooting, you're complaining

the star can't win
if it cannot be accepted as it is
in all its majestic yet sometimes troublesome reality
tell me what good is it being a most precious jewel
in the galaxy?
if even amongst all the others
the star stays afloat
in the dark
desolate and lonely?

cappuccino

the foamy sip
of cappuccino
enters my mouth
gradually
forewarning
either a warm
or
scorching
hot sip

reminding me of foamy waves
approaching the shore
they could wash over me
or swallow me whole
yet alive

I
must
take
a
dip

its cappuccino
foams rising higher and higher
the waves approach me as I rest on the shore
with my body on the wet sand
seashells scratch my hand

the water could indeed swallow me whole
I remind myself once more

or, it could subside as it nears

I'll just have to take my chances
life's full of surprising circumstances

regardless of our tears and fears

sharp communication

mercury is in retrograde
it's your time of the month
you've been having a rough day
I've got a lot of other problems on my mind

it's amazing the excuses we can make
the variety of sources on which
we can shift the blame
for our hurtful or ice-cold words

a single word, or lack of
can singlehandedly create the sharpest knife
reaching down deep
and cutting out the very life and root
of any glimmer of hope, belief, or smile

the knife can carve out
the most excruciatingly painful
and disfigured shape in our hearts
adding unwanted emotions
of anger and nervous regret
to the always welcomed
and pure basis of affinity
upon which we had initially
built our behavioral coziness

we are the choices we make
do we really not see?
we are the creators of our own words
just as we are of our worlds

destiny can play a hand, sure
but astrology?
a bad day?
physical sluggishness?
financial or family issues?
would we use these sources
to blame a murder?

when we don't choose our words carefully
with the most precious and
intimate people in our lives
that is exactly what we commit
we slowly become murderers
murderers of trust
murderers of love

social media mornings

mornings once started
with opening our eyes to peek outside
of our windows
for a glimmer of sunshine behind the clouds
or sounds of raindrops tapping
or heavy gusts of wind-howling
or the gentle whisper
of pristine snow falling

mornings once started
with the desire for some tea, juice or coffee
warm crispy bread toasted
to perfection with butter

mornings once meant curiosity
about real current events
and intellectual stimulation
to activate our minds
sniffing that wonderful print-smell
to flip through the newspaper
or turning on the television to listen
to expert commentaries

mornings now?
still waking up with the desire
to observe, sense, and satiate curiosities
but technology has replaced the weather
taking place outside our windows

social applications
have ingested that cup of coffee
or toast we could smell in our minds
even before they could be prepared

they have even gobbled up
our traditional paperbacks or hardcovers

in the mornings now
we shall be in mourning
for telecommunications are observing us
curious about us
devouring us

duality

she is a peculiar one
they say
her eyes burn dark
but skin caresses soft
like a flower in May

she wears her accumulated adornments loudly
each one reflecting petal off-springs of the rainbow

yet her wide-brimmed ebony hat
and clothes remain fixed proudly

if not for the darkness
the master thinks
how would all my prisms show?

woman

                                                  girl

wakes up, looks out the window
tall buildings' chauffeur starting up
the Ferrari to drive her to school
maid cleaning up after her breakfast
of scrambled eggs and French toast
all the other girls envy her

                                                  girl

lonely inside

                                                  girl

wakes up, looks out the window
gets out the door of the car
mother sleeps in the driver's seat
goes next to mom to wake her up
to ask her where they will be looking for a
home and breakfast
that particular foggy morning

                                                  girl

hope in her heart

girl

    wakes up, her friends, the ants and bugs
    crawling on the street, tell her
    good morning
    needs to find her younger brother
    they need to somehow escape yet into
    another city in hopes of surviving
    that day's awaited bomb

girl

tears in her eyes

girl

    wakes up, turns on the T.V.
    watches the news, thinking about
    how she could make a difference for the better
    picks up her homework
    meets up with her friend
    as they walk to class that day

girl

determination in her soul

girl

give her a chance, listen to her, care for her

girl

don't let anyone undermine
your beauty and intelligence

girl

take charge, make a difference
help those around you

girl

use whatever you have, whether it is your money
your willpower or your heart
and do something good with it

girl

know that you deserve to be listened to
appreciated and respected

girl

have faith, and know
that no matter what you're going through
you will learn from your experiences and blossom
into a magnificent and strong being:
a loving, caring, intelligent, smiling
through her tears, loved

woman

Drops of Music

rappin' for Queens

Aces of Spades
the ladies of Queens
brave Kings of Diamonds
who'd go to extremes
the borough holds all flags
from Peruvian to Chinese hubs
the most diverse in the Nation
its people dance their souls in clubs

picket fences look at co-ops
juxtaposed industrial
commercial and residential
I became a true American here
to my hometown I remain partial

the most loyal of Queens
you welcomed me in '92
thank you
my borough remains forever youthful
in all its residents' hearts
no others can compare to you
for you do you

senses

listen
only to that voice inside
ignore unsympathetic whispers
trying to exert control
you know your melody
the best

they can't know
your spirit
as a whole

keep away
from those
always bellicose
save your own
soul

observe

the eyes
read poetry
the soul
hears a melody
the heart
registers the verses
the spirit
feels music's magical curses

like versus love

this city is made up of bridges
once you're on the path of one
there's no way out
must face the consequences
waiting on the other side
whether you're apathetic
or devout

the city is full of dirty noise
one of many things about it
beyond your control
you must force yourself
to enjoy the fast-pace
even when you're weary
and jaded after it all

you don't like New York
it can never make you feel whole
yet you love it
breathe it
the city where you root
your soul

dancing mermaid

the melodic hymns
of her soul
sometimes take
utter control

like sirens
singing with heavy breaths
luring captains
to their untimely deaths

the music of her heart
possesses her fragile
and tired mind
it won't let her start
another day
with his memory left behind

wishful thinking

I don't know quite when
not sure quite how
vulnerably- catalyzed me
has been able to survive
without crumbling by now

the struggle of trying to always reach out
prove my worth
and instill the same self-confidence
in the other
has often been taken advantage of
as they've drained my pure energy
to recharge their souls
leaving me weaker in my ether
often alone as I later suffer

how much longer can I keep up appearances
of strength and forgiveness
and onward fight?
how much longer can I swallow my tears?
how much longer can I hide my fright
and persevere with might?

may I no longer be forced to smile
as I hide my scream
may I no longer troop on alone

may the nightmares transform into a dream

the thrill of creativity

close your eyes
does it appear underneath your eyelids?
the last time you'd actually aspired
to accomplish a feat?
and not merely go through the motions
of duties obsolete?
aspirations set upon yourself
by your own conscience and will
can you visualize the last time
you've actually felt that natural, authentic thrill?
never let that teenager inside of you
stop dreaming
for when that fire stops burning
we cease growing
and expanding

sober inebriation

summer birthdays
full of bittersweet daze
tears welling up
hidden by the sun's rays

growing younger as we get older
earning wisdom in exchange for
one disappointment
and another

stay strong, my brother
don't sell out, my sister
be drunk on life
while remaining sober

yin and yang

the professional
professor
the nurturing
mother
the majestic
angel
the demonic devil

she can be all she is called
yet she is ultimately none

always a battle persists
one which can never be won

a woman can try to achieve
everything possible under the sun

it remains, regardless of progress
a man's world
for boys are still allowed more fun

the mother

people always have a sense of wonder
when they see a woman standing alone
without another

is she a good one?
or is she a sinner?
is she a free spirit?
or is she a protector?

labels haven't helped anyone
my friend
for in the end
life is simply how you react in the moment
and in particular shoes
when an event summons

we've all got
both our angels
as well as demons

theatrics

if you deny
satiating your soul
for the sake of others

then who are you?
when you can't truly breathe
under masks and covers?

some wear visible masks
only in October

others wear invisible ones
the rest of the year
their various truths hidden
behind a cover

umbrellas
yes, against the raindrops
can provide shelter

while self-defense shields
could certainly
when faced with fate
falter

silenced victims

as he loosens
his buckles
with nervousness- not consent
she chuckles

calculates ways out of her cage
to escape and open a clean page

he purposely ignores her age
as well as her secret rage

she hides her fear
only to have food and shelter near

it's not her choice
please allow her a voice

the fooled teen

glasses, frizz
unpainted fingernails on her hand
a teenage girl
doesn't aim to, nor should she ever
attract a man

adored by those her age
even at her nerdiest
yet the words of the legal adult
had proved to be the cleverest

a predator is hard to notice
when he's given a girl her first real kiss
if there could've been a chance
to do it all over again
she'd have gone to her family or the police station
right there and then

she had bottled up all her rage
to her surprise- today it still spills onto the page
the pain hasn't made her a helpless victim
nor some all-knowing sage
she simply continues to bleed her art
each day can become a new start
and the world truly is her stage

anticipation

I wait for my destiny
to rear its either ugly or stupendous head out
from the blanket of slowly-passing time
under which it's been hiding

I'm not choosy
I wait like the passenger waits for the train
to catch the next appointment with a loved one
a professional opportunity
or disappointment
even with death

I wait, you see
without any supposition

when you feel the call of
destiny
everything else is merely a check-off list
until you can finally feel at peace
at one with your own unique place
in infinity

bare

I will allow the sun to shine
no shades
I will fight for what is mine
no shades

I will brave the feared
I will weather the storm
I will pray to be healed
I will defy the norm

I will be who I am
regardless of grays
I am both the dark and light
throughout all of my days

I will face those rays

the savior

it's indeed strange
how wisdom and
true self-acceptance
only come with age

I'm neither a model
nor an hourglass
I'm a guitar
with strings of brass

I'm not a superstar
nor a CEO
but feel fulfilled
being my own hero

the traveler

the sightseer
thought to be
always seeking
novelty
in reality
seeks conformity
in the innate ability
of people with new visions to see
to welcome with glee
her familiar
eccentricity
however different
they all may be
from one another
in actuality

the protagonist

books
on shelves
describe Santa
more than elves

the prominent
receive prominence
while the aides
are described
only through
their obedience

fair or not
we must play that part
become the protagonist
of your own heart
of your own art

the blind archer

I am a blind archer
captivated by the target
despite a visionless sight

I am the prickliest rose in the orchard
useless for fruit production
though dangerously lovely in the light

I am the messiest neat freak
OCD with symmetry
though cleaning makes me shriek

I am the most exciting bore
The most thrilling wh...chore
I am the craziest sage
insane and wise to my very core

I am the owner of a biography
to make you weep
reading through my roller coaster chapters
you'd finish me
in one sweep

I am the simplest mystery

I am duality, and duality is me

the cat and the soul met

the images provoked in my mind
invoked by a sunset or a sunrise
bring memories of different
people's eyes

I feel like a cat
in that I've already lived through 8 of my lives
and that I'm on my final one
still humorously looking for *the one*

but I now believe- we don't get one soulmate
but rather we get one soul-met
a soul our souls has crossed
during one particular moment

a soul we have simply met
and said *hello* to
through a kiss, a hug, a look, a summer, winter
or a catalyst heartbreak

I've learned not to take any experience
for granted
but to not attach myself to anything either
whatever life sends us
we can take

royal folklore

the ice queen
suffers forced isolation
despite playing like a child
freezing everything during procrastination

the Arabian princess
suffers duties and responsibilities
before Aladdin-family and country
preceded other amorous possibilities

you are my queen, he claims
with eyes begging for more
she sighs, and cannot be flattered
her pristine loyalty to them soon feels like a bore
the happiness of royalty is folklore

hope

they won in the end
a haunting past
and isolated present
for both him and I

he watches now only from afar
and I, like a fool
still have kept my door slightly ajar

hope should sometimes be a sin
for it can allow
either devilish or foolish thoughts
to creep in

yet other times I get confused
and I feel it to my bones
for the accumulation over time
of the smallest glitters of hope
can also erode
even the hardest of stones

the peace

a piece of chocolate
melted in the mouth
as if the cocoa has the power
to manipulate brain cells
into believing all will be well

a piece of information
ingested with utmost curiosity and satisfaction
if originating from a source of someone
who makes you feel swell

a peace of mind
is the rarest jewel to discover
and be able to spread throughout the mind
for it is the only one
the soul needs to survive
the success or failure of which
only time can tell

the floater

life often provides
timely signs ignored
yet recognized
in retrospect
you actively live
in the moment
not fully utilizing
your head

harsh consequences
however
can ultimately haunt
the adult
floating like a teenager
void of responsibility
some haven't fully
grasped this yet

if it makes you smile in a moment
all later pain
we tend to forget
under a pretense of
no regret

dear new year

dear tomorrow
could you please help me overcome
all of my inner sorrow?

can each anxiety attack
alongside of OCD
I conceal
finally become appeased
through a sense of belonging
and settlement
with just a dash of zeal?

can you help me
to help myself?
to do so but still
be myself?
sounds like a silly thing to ask
but self-acceptance
in implementation
is truly a difficult task

pink means go

when you have to be given the green light
go pink
go your own way
resist that traumatically-bonded
pull to stay

don't overthink

if they had been
true blue
a real one, through and through

you would have felt welcomed from the start
anyway
permission isn't needed
to be yourself
on any day

the variation of violence

knives on the street
punches and slaps indoors
we can hurt life rivals
as cruelly as the ones we claim to love the most
and we wonder why
the human race still can't prevent wars

the monsters within
often wait for the next opportunity
lurking beneath the skin
desiring confrontation
in close proximity

we must choose our words
even more carefully
than our battles
and swords
karma chases heart-crackers
as well as those folks
who remain cement-hard
and bellicose

the shield of humor

the
fake
snake
in the lake
made my body shake

tremors and panic attacks
caused by surprise tricks
hurt the most when one lacks
self-defense against stones and sticks

feigned
love
feels ordained
from above

until harsh reality pokes
suddenly you'd prefer the jokes

the officer

faithfully
I execute my task

the dutiful officer
of fulfilling an expectation

of countless subjects
without much protest or sensation

if I've reaped any benefits as well
they never ask

'Sel'

August 8, 1984
a baby-unwanted by her father
came into this world
she's a gift
he'd told his wife that Wednesday
you wanted a baby so much
the *gift* would grow up
without knowing a father's
protective touch

growing up amongst duality
of clashing cultures and her own personality
she was always searching
the 8-8
soul-eaters fed off of her energy
you're a princess they all said
yet in regards to what she needed
they could care less
and did not appreciate
or
genuinely reciprocate

November 25, 2015
her world changed
she'd no longer act like a teen
motherhood didn't develop
as planned and arranged
life became simpler yet serene

my rock

she is my rock
she keeps me grounded
both sweet and adventurous
she's quite well-rounded

she's my daughter after all
she's not always a picnic
but still is my closest ally
as God must have intended

she can make me smile through my tears
I can't always comprehend it
I've had so many more downs than ups
but somehow still
I can be made to feel
that I've made it

the foam's advice

where is my Captain?
the mermaid asked
he's been captured after the vessel's shipwreck
the foams answered

what do I do now?
she whimpered

float on rough waters
by continuously flipping your own tail
and turn the tide in your own favor
the foams encouraged
he may be gone, but you can be your own Savior

humility

colorful books
stacked before a
hand-print marked
window sill
exist now more for art
whereas reading
had once been
my daily pill

she used to nap
and I would smile
a book could distract me
for a while
now my toddler pouts
when I'm without her
in her young life
she's been through
much grief and many
goodbyes to incur

she's my entertainment now
and humbly I'm grateful
a child's a blessing
many wish for, so
perhaps that's more
beautiful

maternal guilt

on these cruel
city streets
I can be exhausted
to the max
yet I'll still carry her
if she needs me to
they say *let us help you relax*
but it's me
whose eyes she implores
for it's me
whom she thinks sometimes ignores
not knowing my heart
explodes, and explores
ways to make up to her
all of my shortcomings
and the patience
my spirit lacks

birthday woman-child part 1

this is 35
what you don't know is that in my family
no one has really lived past the age of 70
and so I would be considered midlife already
that is, if I'm even lucky
for trauma always pursues me relentlessly
my biological father himself died at 50
so what could possibly await me?
only God knows the reality
but I'll keep dancing to my own tune
and suffer fools gladly
as long as I can be there
for my baby

birthday woman-child part 2

this is 36
too many words
have hurt more than sticks

a dream admired
six figures desired
but my weary soul is getting tired

a prisoner of circumstance
stuck between conscience and chance

double standards
hypocrisy
no more highs
off of pointless jealousy
phantoms who lead to nowhere
just leave me be

I feel more loved on my own
than by words verbally expressed
but never shown

medea

you are my sunshine
I sang to you, before you were even born
I had been amongst strict military crowds
feeling misplaced, and rather forlorn

you developed and came so peacefully
wrapping your fingers around my pointer
I had unpreparedly become
something much idolized
I'd become a mother

with its good and bad
life as we knew it changed in one night
despite innocence we were displaced
yet history will write the truth, and the schemers
will become the ones disgraced

just as we've gotten comfortable
with our new order
attempting peace through the chaos
of our new shelter
old demons re-emerge
and if they try to take away
our sunshine together?
hell indeed have no fury
like a scorned child-bearer
I'll let that thought linger

the biggest fan

and in this life
you may turn out to be
my only real fan
and my only real friend
yet in the end
I'll fight on alone
if I have to
with or without a plan
or a man
for it is you
I can never reprimand
for you always understand
as long as I live
I will never let go of your hand

socio-political genocide

rotting away in boxes
is my only settled life
one I'd barely gotten to know
with the role of a dutiful wife

I search for my baggy sweater
without him too, I feel bare
like the coziness of dear packed-away furniture
it also just isn't there

must be in one of the killed-memory
holders of cardboard

forced evacuation
shunned by half a nation
will any of us reunite?
it too remains unclear
I'll maintain a sense of
settlement
as a vagabond
in this new role I've found
praying for justice
year after year

bloodline tears

red, red eyes
blood-red eyes
painfully-pink eyes
they cannot disguise
they cannot pretend
that they've poured for some hurtful friend
for in the end
It's the most painful downpour, you see
when your tears have fallen due to family

some bridges are meant to be crossed
some are meant to be burned
some connect briefly
while others are earned

at the end of this one, which I'm on
I realize now, I can see

that it is only she
who alone with compassion and understanding
is waiting for me
she is neither my mother
my warm-looking mother with words of stone
nor my daughter
my untimely yet beautiful source
of motivation to go on

she is my future reflection
She is me
and she alone is no one

red-next-morning puffy eyes
they attempt to disguise
a mentally-abusive lover
a proud vessel whom the world
only sees the surface of on the water
unaware of the painful propeller

my tears
have been my truest lifelong friend
to them I will now respectfully add humility
as we continue to walk that bridge
until the very end

hero nostalgia

nostalgic songs
haunt me from the radio
I used to reminisce
smile
and then let it go

been getting harder and harder
however
to do that, you know
for too many sunsets have passed
and soon it will again be time for snow

my loneliness becoming increasingly highlighted
even in a crowd
longing to be more
than my own fellow, my own beau
I still yearn for a hero
guess I need to be my own, though

unappeasable expectations

the heaviness on her shoulders
could not be appeased
by any soft massage done at the salon
those shoulders can't heal with a squeeze
regardless of how much she needs
another's to lean on

she's taken on the sins of her father
who has been long gone
but whose betrayal still haunts her mother
her fiery eyes turn to his in her eyes
each time the girl confronts another

despite the new generation that has arrived
the burden still will not let go
a daughter who has miraculously
survived
shouldn't suffer for the sins of her father
this- the grandparent now has simply got to know

when you can't write, dance it out

the best part of parenthood
so far
has been being given a second chance
a do-over
to re-witness every single endeavor of life
from the exquisite to the irksome
and view it from the outside in
like a moviegoer
children don't change
just age
lives rearrange
do we fit on the same page?
separate the fool from the sage
sometimes we belong in a cage
I'm more than my rage
thoughts...thoughts...thoughts
hush!
stillness
I throw my child a glance
I'm an angel before the fall again
with purity I shall dance

write out your drops

the ocean asks
for your drops of rain
the lover says *cry me a river*
whether of joy or of pain

the future asks for your blood drops
for you to contribute your genetically-inherited art
bleed out your art
bleed it out, through your heart

symphonies ask for your melodic drops
success asks for your hard work
your perspiration drops
the struggle never stops

go ahead, ride out the storm
you can keep warm
as long as you write out your drops

epilogue

when faced with the unknown
your inner voice and light
are sometimes the only paths shown
before the advent of technology
a lighthouse- a star on earth- was shone
showing boats
in the ocean
home
despite standing alone

the ripple effect
or
butterfly one
somehow, it's all been coined
and done

yet clichés exist for a reason
they hold true through every season

we are all a mere drop in that ocean
you see
we shan't hold back any story
that will one day become history
for collectively, we are the human community
we are family

About the Author

SELIN SENOL-AKIN, a New Yorker and academic, has been a storyteller ever since she was selected to represent her local Queens public school in a citywide *Storytelling* contest at the tender age of 9, just one year after immigrating to the United States.

She's published her first poem in high school and went on to write academic/journalistic articles for several local magazines and newspapers. With advanced degrees and certification in both Political Science/ International Relations, as well as TESOL/ ESL education- she's also been involved in the performing arts as a hobby.

Selin has read her poetry at annual NYC events like *Pynk* and the multi-national *Versos Estivales* Poetry Festival, where her work was included in the published anthology of the same name along with other accomplished poets. Her short story, "Ordinary" (about child abuse) was featured in the feminist anthology *Flash* and she was furthermore chosen as a featured poet to represent Queens at the popular open-mic showcase "Inspired Word."

Her debut suspense novel, *The Catalyst,* made its way onto becoming a #1 New Release online, despite being first published at the onset of the pandemic, and will soon be re-released as a part of a Trilogy of the same name.

https://www.selinsenolakin.com/

www.ingramcontent.com/pod-product-compliance
Lightning Source LLC
Chambersburg PA
CBHW071501080526
44587CB00014B/2177